Plesiosaurus

Written by Rupert Oliver
Illustrated by Andrew Howatt

Library of Congress Cataloging in Publication Data

Oliver, Rupert.
  Plesiosaurus.

  Summary: A day in the life of a plesiosaurus, an air-
breathing, prehistoric, marine reptile, as she lays eggs,
escapes other predators, searches for food, and fights a
storm at sea.
  1. Plesiosaurus—Juvenile literature.   [1. Plesiosaurus.
2. Prehistoric animals]   I. Title.
QE862.P4044   1984   567.9'3   84-16095
ISBN 0-86592-211-X

Rourke Enterprises, Inc.
Vero Beach, FL 32964

Rhamphorhynchus

Pteranodon

Pterodactyl

Ankylosaurus

Dimetrodon

Iguanodon

Tricondon

Plesiosaurus

Archaeopteryx

Ichthyosaurus

Plesiosaurus

Deinonychus

Nothosaurus

The sun sparkled on the waves and the surf crashed on the beach. A cool breeze rippled the surface of the warm, sun drenched sea. Suddenly a long neck rose up from the water. On top of the snake like neck was a small head. Plesiosaurus had come to lay her eggs.

Plesiosaurus eyed the broad beach carefully. There was often danger on the beach. Plesiosaurus could only see a group of Cetiosaurus and Pelorosaurus on the beach. Such plant eating dinosaurs were no danger to Plesiosaurus, so she began to lumber up on to the beach. Plesiosaurus used her strong flippers to drag herself over the sand. She was not very agile and was always clumsy on land.

Plesiosaurus lumbered over the warm sand. The sun quickly dried her skin. When Plesiosaurus was above the high tide mark she began to dig. She knew that her eggs would be safest if she buried them in the sand. Hunting animals would be less likely to find them and the sand would help to keep them warm.

Plesiosaurus worked busily with her front
flippers. Her flippers were really built for swimming
not for digging. After a time she had dug a hole
which was deep enough. Plesiosaurus turned around
and began to lay her eggs. The sand near to
Plesiosaurus suddenly began to move. There was
something under the sand trying to get out.

Plesiosaurus finished laying her eggs. She used her hind flippers to cover the eggs with the warm sand. She had only just finished when a terrible roar boomed across the beach.

Looking round in alarm, Plesiosaurus saw a pair of Megalosaurs at the edge of the forest. The fierce meateaters had seen Plesiosaurus. They began to run towards her. Plesiosaurus knew what would happen if these dinosaurs caught her. Her life was in danger.

Plesiosaurus dragged herself across the beach as fast as she could. She knew that if she could reach the water she would be safe. All the time the ferocious hunters were catching up with Plesiosaurus. She was very frightened. The pounding feet of the bellowing Megalosaurs were close behind. At last Plesiosaurus reached the water. She swam off leaving the hunters on the shore.

As Plesiosaurus watched a small head broke
the surface of the sand. Then another head appeared.
The heads were followed by tiny Plesiosaurus. They
belonged to the eggs of another Plesiosaurus which
had laid her eggs on the beach a few weeks earlier.
Soon there were dozens of baby Plesiosaurus on the
beach. They all began to crawl towards the ocean.
Then from out of the sky, a Rhamphorhynchus
swooped down. It grabbed a baby Plesiosaurus in its
jaws and flew off.

Other Rhamphorhynchus arrived and began to eat the babies. From the forest a Teinurosaurus appeared and dashed across the beach. Soon it too, was gobbling up the babies. Eventually about half the babies reached the safety of the sea. When Plesiosaurus's eggs hatched her young would have to face the same dangerous journey to the sea.

Plesiosaurus was glad to be back in the water. This was where she felt at home. The waves lapped over her body as she paddled out to sea. With strong, even strokes Plesiosaurus moved across the water surface. Now that she had laid her eggs, Plesiosaurus realized that she was hungry.

With her head held high Plesiosaurus could see a large area of ocean. A sudden flash of silver caught Plesiosaurus's eye. There was a school of fish just beneath the surface. Plesiosaurus gently paddled towards the fish. When she was close enough Plesiosaurus darted her head forward. Her jaws plunged into the water and emerged with a fish. Plesiosaurus quickly gobbled down the fish. Then her head struck out again and she caught another fish.

Suddenly Plesiosaurus realized that there
were some creatures beneath her that were not fish.
They looked like fish, but they were far larger. Then
two of the creatures burst out of the water. They were
Ichthyosaurs.

Just beneath the surface of the sea the
Ichthyosaurs dashed to and fro snapping up the fish
as fast as they could. Before long the fish had
scattered in all directions. The Ichthyosaurus moved
on in search of more fish. Plesiosaurus was still
hungry. She also would have to find more food.

The waves on the ocean were becoming larger and the wind was getting stronger. After a while Plesiosaurus was having to paddle up and down the waves because they were so large. Plesiosaurus was still looking for food, but she could not find any more fish.

As Plesiosaurus looked around a gigantic
head burst through the water. The great jaws were
filled with teeth and were almost half the size of
Plesiosaurus's entire body. Plesiosaurus was
frightened and began to swim off as fast as she could.
The great head disappeared back beneath the water.
When it reappeared the jaws were firmly grasping
several cuttlefish. The giant beast was a Pliosaur.
Plesiosaurus knew that the newcomer was no real
danger to her. All this time dark clouds had been
gathering and the waves had been getting larger and
stronger. A storm was brewing.

In a very short time dark clouds had covered the entire sky and the wind had become a screaming gale. The waves towered over Plesiosaurus as she struggled to stay upright. One particular wave came crashing down on top of Plesiosaurus. The great weight of water entirely covered Plesiosaurus. Under the water Plesiosaurus could not breathe and she tried desperately to reach the surface again. Eventually she was able to take a breath of air.

High above Plesiosaurus, lightning flashed from cloud to cloud. Thunder rumbled out across the sky. Plesiosaurus was very frightened indeed. The gigantic waves continued to lash against her and the wind howled around her.

After many hours the wind became weaker. The huge, dark clouds drifted away and the sky was clear again. Soon the waves were smaller. The sea was almost calm. Plesiosaurus was able to swim without any difficulty. She sighted a school of fish and swam over to them. As her head dipped into the water to grab a fish, another animal flashed by. The fish were being hunted by a Metriorhynchus as well as by Plesiosaurus.

The Metriorhynchus took a few fish and then swam on. Plesiosaurus was left alone on the wide open sea. After a while she began eating fish again. She would have to build up her strength after fighting the terrible storm.

Plesiosaurus and the Late Jurassic Oceans

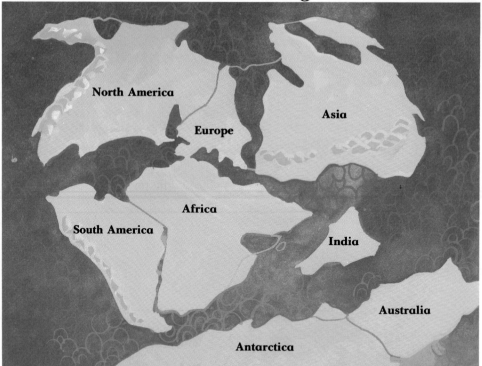

North America

Europe

Asia

Africa

South America

India

Australia

Antarctica

**This is a map of the world in Late Jurassic times.
The continents were in quite different places, as you can see. The Plesiosaurus
in the book lived in the sea to the left, or west, of Europe.**

When did Plesiosaurus live?

Plesiosaurus lived during the Age of the Dinosaurs. Known to scientists as the Mesozoic Era, the Age of the Dinosaurs began about 225 million years ago and ended about 65 million years ago. This immense stretch of time has been divided into three periods – the Triassic, the Jurassic and the Cretaceous. Plesiosaurus lived toward the end of the Jurassic, approximately 150 million years ago. Different types of plesiosaur lived right up to the end of the Age of Dinosaurs.

Where did Plesiosaurus live?

Fossils of different types of plesiosaur have been found in many parts of the world. It would seem that the plesiosaurs were a very successful group of animals which lived in all the seas of the world at the same time. The plesiosaurs in the book lived in shallow seas off the coasts of western Europe. All the animals in the book also lived in the same seas at the same time. Plesiosaurs living in other seas at other times would have encountered different animals in their lives.

The Discovery of Plesiosaurus

For millions of years the fossilized bones of the plesiosaurs lay below the sea floor. Later the rocks in which they lay were forced up by the titanic earth movements and became dry land. People then sometimes discovered the fossils but not until a mere hundred years ago did scientists learn about the giant reptiles of the Mesozoic.

Plesiosaurus may have been the very first giant reptile whose bones were found and studied. Hundreds of years ago, long before scientists had found out about dinosaurs and other giant reptiles, some strange bones were found in Germany. At that time, people thought that the bones belonged to winged dragons with long necks. The people who found the bones drew pictures of what they thought the dragons had looked like. If the wings in these drawings are replaced with flippers, the 'dragons' look very much like plesiosaurs. Scientists now think that the 'dragon bones' were really fossilized plesiosaur skeletons. In recent times plesiosaur skeletons have been found in the same part of Germany. One of the first complete plesiosaur skeletons to be discovered, was found more than a hundred years ago in England by a young girl called Mary Anning. Plesiosaurs have, therefore, been known to science for quite a long time.

The evolution of the Plesiosaurs

Though plesiosaurs lived during the Mesozoic Era, the Age of the Dinosaurs, they were not actually dinosaurs. The ancestors of the plesiosaurs belonged to a group which had produced the ten foot long Nothosaurus, some sixty million years earlier. Nothosaurus, and its relatives, were the most important type of reptile in the seas of the Triassic period. They had strong legs, unlike the flippers of Plesiosaurus, and spent much of their time on the land. It would seem that the nothosaurs were halfway along the evolutionary trail from a land reptile to a sea reptile, such as Plesiosaurus. By studying the fossilized skeletons of nothosaurs and plesiosaurs, scientists can discover many things. One of these is that the two groups belonged to a single, larger group. Indeed, it is possible that plesiosaurs were descended from nothosaurs.

At the beginning of the Jurassic period, about 190 million years ago, the line of the plesiosaurs split in two. Some plesiosaurs evolved long necks and small heads, others evolved short necks and long heads. Plesiosaurus, itself, was a member of the first group. The long-necked group culminated in the 45 foot long Elasmosaurus which lived in the Cretaceous period.

If the long-necked plesiosaurs were large animals, their short-necked relatives became enormous. Pliosaurus, whose enormous head frightened the Plesiosaurus in our story, was a short-necked species. One kind, known as Kronosaurus, had a head twice as long as a man is tall, and measured fiftyfive feet in length. Plesiosaurus was part of a very large family tree. Despite their numbers all the plesiosaurs and pliosaurs became extinct before the end of the Cretaceous period.

Other Reptiles of the Jurassic

Plesiosaurus was a very common type of reptile in the Jurassic seas, but there were many other kinds of reptile alive at the same time. The land was dominated by three groups of dinosaur. The most important plant-eaters were the enormous sauropods. Cetiosaurus and Pelorosaurus were both types of Sauropod and were both more than sixty feet long. The smaller hunters were Coelurosaurs, such as Teinurosaurus which can be seen making a meal of the baby Plesiosaurs on pages 10 and 11. The most powerful hunters of all were the carnosaurs. The thirty foot long Megalosaurus was a type of carnosaur.

Although reptiles first evolved on the land, many returned to the sea. Plesiosaurus was one of these. The ichthyosaurs were perhaps best adapted to life in the sea. These reptiles had evolved a body which was very fish-like in appearance and was ideally suited to a swimming life. Unlike plesiosaurs, the ichthyosaurs could not go ashore to lay their eggs and had to give birth at sea like whales and dolphins today. Metriorhynchus was a sea crocodile, literally a crocodile that took to a life at sea. Despite these adaptations the sea crocodiles died out within a few million years. At the time of our story, flying reptiles such as Rhamphorhynchus still ruled the air, although the first birds had already evolved.

Nothosaurus. Length: 9 feet.

Elasmosaurus. Length: 45 feet